Make Time

for the

Spiritual

Joseph Raffa

Make Time for the Spiritual

Author: Joseph Raffa

Editor: Teena Raffa-Mulligan

ISBN 978-0-9944990-3-5

eISBN 978-0-9944990-6-6

Author's note: The term 'mankind' as used throughout this discourse is a reference to the human race collectively.

Published by Sea Song Publications

sea-song@bigpond.com

www.seasongpublications.com

~1~

ECONOMIC DEVELOPMENT AS a means to improve the quality of life and supply the needs of an expanding population is being pursued with almost religious zeal worldwide. Rarely do we find any place on this planet where humans live that is not touched in some way by the restless tide of progress and change.

A great deal of energy and effort are being applied to make living on this planet as comfortable, as varied and as secure as it can be. Innovation is the name of the game. Changes do not have to be urgently needed to become part of day to day living. It is enough if imaginative minds create an appetite for the products presented to those who are drawn to whatever is new.

The mind has not yet reached saturation point after years of accelerating progress in material productivity. Development and acquisition, whatever the scale, is of vital importance to the human psyche.

People expand and develop with their possessions. They gain considerable standing in their own or others' eyes by owning or by being involved in projects of importance. Spectacular projects that offer much are announced with a fanfare of publicity. Expectations are fuelled about their community value and the excitement is contagious. Impressive plans are formulated and colourful advertising is circulated to advise the public about new ventures. Where new housing estates are the theme, these are presented with an enhanced atmosphere to stimulate desire to live in the area.

All this makes the thoughtful wonder — why does human value apparently increase as possessions or production increase? Why is achievement looked on as the gateway to superiority in living, as the measuring stick that determines the success or otherwise of human endeavour? There is a reaching out in so many ways to gain greater distinction. It is obviously important to reach the top, to own homes and land in valued areas, to have material possessions, to identify with something greater than we take ourselves to be. Or there is involvement with patterns and lifestyles that supply enhanced meaning to life.

Emptiness is dreaded. Inaction, not being related to happenings that stimulate or satisfy, can drive us restlessly onwards to search amidst the social surrounds for something to come to ground in that complements a deep psychological need to stand out or gain a measure of fulfilment. Society and what it offers is where many go in the search for something worthwhile. In its organisations, its variable offerings, we expect to find something somewhere that will hold the attention and supply what is needed, mentally, emotionally and physically.

We wander the highways and byways of our social surrounds, exploring and savouring the array on display in the marketplace of timeful experience. When one thing fails to satisfy the needs of the moment, we move on to something else. Why the relentless drive for self-fulfilment? We have appetites that demand to be fed. Even if the demand is only for a constant variety of experiences to absorb the surface attention. The self dances to the tune of insistent drives. It surges out into the social surrounds, to find there something that will clothe its restless desires in acceptable meaning and enhanced living.

Humans feel naked and alone without identification, involvement and achievement. We fill our lives with action along chosen lines of behaviour and social involvement, otherwise we feel worthless, dissatisfied and unfulfilled. There is a seeking of greater importance for the self through achievement, ownership and identification. While the self is contented with a return that lifts its estimation of its worth, it will go on directing energy and attention along pathways that yield a psychological return of security and inner reassurance. The desire to gain inwardly can be a compelling force for action through adulthood. Fed with attention and energy, it operates unhindered to be a dominant influence in the human expression.

Outward tuned as it is, the mind is unaware of the inner nature of the complex drives that direct the individual momentum on its way through the social surrounds. Because of the ready identification with and acceptance of these basic traits in behaviour — through the desires and demands that follow and focus on what we want to do and have — there is little resistance to the flow of the inner trends into the outer world. Resistance may in fact breed a greater determination to have our way and if too powerful may lead to resentment if our intentions are obstructed. Rarely do we set out to explore behaviour, preferring to accept it without investigation. We consider what we are and what we do our private business and insist we should be able, within reasonable limits to do what we want with our lives.

This deeply held attitude makes it difficult to unravel the ins and outs of what is going on in this troublesome little mind of ours. The self's tenacity to hold on and persevere with its convictions and intentions is remarkable. While it is so wholeheartedly committed to serving its own interests it is not going to allow any suggestion to intrude that it would be wiser to take a good, long look at what it is doing and thinking before it acts in well-defined directions. The self finds it easier to browse along life's highway, serving its likes, desires and demands, spinning its web of interrelated activity, looking for favourable returns. Sooner or later, however, it bumps into pain or disturbance. Perhaps then it shifts into an introspective gear to determine if it can what went wrong with its approach. The intention is to avoid painful and unpleasant experiences and get back to normal without unduly changing the self's basic makeup. We do kind of love what we are and in spite of the acknowledgement that our behaviour is not the best at times or what it should be, still we are accustomed to how we express ourselves and inclined to look on this with favourable judgement.

Seeing we are so self-centred, set in our ways and do not want to shift out of the familiar grooves the self has forged for itself, why is it that spiritually enlightened people come amongst us and gently knock on our mental doors in a bid to awaken a new direction in living and learning? Do they just want to make a nuisance of themselves? Do they seek some kind of inner fulfilment? Have they the wellbeing of their fellow human beings at heart as the driving force that moves them in this unusual way? Undoubtedly some, even though they clothe their intentions in fine-sounding words, are mainly serving the self in some way. But are all those who walk across the spiritual stage in this category or are some the willing instruments of a higher love? Are they moved by a wisdom beyond the mind's understanding, yet one they obey without question? In this way they remain true to the nature they have integrated with — the universal whose directives insist on an outlet into the world of everyday human affairs, where others not so enlightened would prefer to be left to their own devices, living life according to the dictates of the little self they have allowed themselves to become anchored in.

The trouble is, without universal integration, difficulties can turn into nasty drawn out affairs that devastate areas of the earth and destroy millions of people's lives before they pass on leaving disturbing psychological and physical legacies. These are not easy happenings to ignore and while all the commotion is going on, the more thoughtful wonder why humans behave in this way and what can be done to avoid a repetition or even worse. Perhaps this is why those who speak from the spiritual side of life come into the picture.

When things are going badly for the human race, then ears are inclined to be more sensitive to the spoken word and the mind more inclined to listen to a new offering, to an invitation to explore the human expression on all the levels on which it functions. Why then, the need for this kind of exploration? In what way is it profitable? Without major disruptions, behaviour, convictions and whatever else has been acquired along the way are taken pretty much for granted. The self understands the returns it gains from the offerings on display in the social marketplace. From a surface standpoint self-discovery does not appear to offer concrete returns.

Yet the thoughtful may well concede that much of what takes place on the surface is a reflection of the inner content the self has accumulated on its timeful journey. What we are capable of doing, for whatever purpose, we will inevitably do regardless of the consequences if the desire is strong. So if investigation of the self's behaviour leads to a deeper understanding of the inner content, its motivations and the thinking processes that emanate from it, then by all means shouldn't this be undertaken without delay? Surely understanding is the key that improves behaviour and dissolves misconceptions. Certainly we will not gain insight into what is going on nor shift from the present mode of doing and thinking by ignoring the inner side of our nature. This side of the human expression has the capacity to initiate responses and actions in apparent disregard of surface intentions. The firmest disciplinary impositions are brushed aside with ease if the inner insists that the outcome shall be otherwise than what the conscious mind decrees.

The difficulty in approaching the inner is that this side of the self's movement is not consciously laid out like the surface aspects in well-defined manner, easy to identify and name. Here, there is not an appearance that can be explored at leisure. It is not like this. Perhaps that is why the psychologist has given this extent the name *unconscious* or *subconscious*, because to the conscious mind it seems to be a rather hazy and indefinite area to move into. Even to name it as an extent or sphere of influence conjures a vista of special characteristics or a substantial location of some kind. Mind loves to think in terms of space and time location with definitions thrown in.

What doesn't match the mind's understanding isn't considered of consequence. It can't help doing this. Such is the way of thought — to deal in thoughtful substance. It has been doing this since its early stages on the planet, that is, dealing with substance, with tangible imprints and suchlike. It is no wonder then that in its approach to learning it needs a tangible image to focus on. Without this it is lost in the ungraspable. Back then to what is referred as the unconscious. What makes humans so certain of its existence inasmuch that it cannot be readily identified as we do with surface phenomena? Come to think of it, although we talk rather easily of *mind*, neither can we isolate and identify what we mean by this word. When it comes to thinking and feeling we are on safer ground. We can observe these activities in progress as they move before the surface attention. This is the evidence of their existence.

For *mind* we may settle on the definition that it is what is responsible for thinking and perceiving and leave it at that, But we are rather puzzled about what its nature is when not involved in activity of any kind. What then would be its definition so the description raises certainty in the mind of another? This would surely be a matter of experiencing rather than explaining. What is beyond surface observation hasn't the usual terms of reference.

There is the same trouble in coming to grips with the unconscious. We take this to mean something that exists in its own right, related intimately to the surface but which is not consciously observed. In this, happenings, whatever is initiated are not broken up like surface experience with a central observer (the mind) and a surrounding sea of effects. The senses do not operate to pick up unconscious activity. The frequencies are beyond them. They haven't the right kind of antennae, being created for specific purposes for which they are admirably suited.

We are not dealing with specifics in approaching the unconscious. This side is an integral part of the human expression, as important as the surface aspect. It shouldn't be ignored because of the difficulties involved in a closer investigation. The unconscious yields evidence of its nature and influence when the conscious and its position of dominance are put aside. Otherwise, as long as the conscious functions at full alert, it continues to hold the centre stage of attention. In so doing, it continues to function on the accustomed level. This is not the level of the unconscious and does not permit this deeper side to show its nature. It is much like being wide awake all the time. Sleep doesn't get a chance to take over.

Is this emphasis on the unconscious necessary in learning about the self? After all, the conscious aspects of existence are readily accessible. Why not leave the other to the experts who study this side and then read the results in the latest books? Yet inasmuch that the surface side we identify with is uniquely our own, so too is the unconscious that relates to it. What takes place does not happen between the pages of a book but within the field of awareness. This intricate interplay between the sensitivity that observes and the surrounding environment, including people — this marvellous response that we know as the human expression in action — must be observed from moment to moment as it arises if we are to understand this process that is the self in movement.

Here a measure of distinction is necessary. The understanding referred to is total in its comprehension, not limited to a reason by reason process dependent on the use of thinking based on words and images with a correlate meaning supplied by the self. It is a remarkably clear seeing that sparkles with insight, brushing aside a reasonable approach or the need for experimentation to unravel the mystery of the self's behaviour. It does not tell us about the intricacies of cell structure or how atoms are arranged. This is the domain of the scientist. It does yield deep and penetrating insights into the hidden side of human nature that cannot be uncovered otherwise. Not even with the use of complex instruments. Even these are dependent on logical reason for their operation and for the interpretation of the data provided.

The learning referred to is a natural arisal from within. It is not acquired from without, from a step by step study of a course imparted by a proficient teacher. Those versed in spiritual matters give a measure of help in unfolding this deeper understanding. This only goes so far, then the seeker is left to go it alone. The dawning of understanding comes without pre-experience. Its impact is like that of a tidal wave at times. We are awash with understanding and by its light we penetrate effortlessly into the underlying aspects of the self at that moment. The conscious has been put aside and the unconscious has revealed some of its content.

~2~

WHAT BRINGS THIS new learning? Is it born of the mind's attempts to gain knowledge from its inward journey? Is it merely the accumulation of new experience that can be cast in the mould of a technical approach and passed on to others as a background for personal use by those inclined to pursue the matter of self-discovery? Mind is eager to impel itself along a reassuring pathway that will lead it into the new fields of self-discovery. It understands motion initiated by itself. It finds it difficult to accept that the most important learning arises when the self as effort and distraction is put aside. Then it happens, unexpectedly — manna from Heaven as the saying goes. Its source — integration with the universal. The release comes from the moment when self is out of the way and the universal is abroad.

Mind generates wear and tear, the to and fro movement of reason, the why this and why that. Then comes the response of analytical thinking as it seeks to provide an understandable answer to the problem that confronts it. What it cannot do for itself it expects an expert to do for it. In matters of self-discovery it turns to spiritual teachers to lead it into new discoveries about self, God and the universe — even how to live and behave. This works well enough in the fields of action and knowledge that relate to the social surrounds. We can learn about these. But the ways of the mind pose difficulties. This is a no go area to anyone else but ourselves. We are in touch here. This is private, our very special precinct.

Here, we walk alone into what we are and do. You may say that God as the universal witness is with us every step of the way but that is a different matter. Whatever the business going on, be it boredom, loneliness, whatever the trend of thinking, the flow of feeling, good or bad, we are right in there with it, setting up the action, shaping the outcome and projecting the finished version onto a conscious screen for final viewing. Self is actor, director and producer, script writer too. The scenario is the life that's lived, day by day. Experience is the background scenery, ever changing.

The curtain rises at the moment of birth. Even before that the body is restlessly on the move, stirring in the darkness of the womb. The fledgling consciousness stirs fitfully, not yet able to crystalise clear meaning from the experiences taking place. With the passage of time and the development of the surface consciousness, self takes off with greater energy. The sense of awareness sharpens and the mind comes into clearer focus with its surrounds. Seeing, feeling, hearing, the action of the senses — this is the machinery set into motion. Through this we come into contact with the body and the outer world.

How we fly the skyways of timeful experience. The colourful scenery fully absorbs the attention and draws the self on a long trail of action and involvement. Now it plays in the garden of sensual delights enfolded by a visually changing panorama. In the centre, beautifully enmeshed with the body so that distinction is difficult to discern, is a strange sensitivity. Through the body — a walking, talking, listening, thinking and feeling response — action and interaction flows in and out with almost lightning-like speed; purposefully channelled, unified and directed, on the lookout for whatever the inner sensitivity desires.

The taste for pleasant sensations to feed the needs and demands of the self is the basis that draws the sensitivity to sift amidst the experiences of time. Here, in the ebb and flow of timeful happenings it attaches itself to ideas, social patterns for living, material possessions and mental constructs that offer worthwhile returns. Impelled by a powerful desire to establish itself, it surges into its surrounds to clothe itself in some form of psychological and material security. Self-protection, survival, expansion and establishment of the self is its main preoccupation. So, the sensitivity settles into time and surrounds like a chicken nestling under the mother hen's protective body.

Here it would stay throughout its earthly life, undisturbed for preference, making itself as comfortable as possible and enjoying the scenery until it is time to go. Nor can it be bothered with difficult questions that invite constant reflection on the whys and wherefores of life, including its own existence. So it buries itself in the sands of time, hoping meanwhile that suffering, torment and the like will pass on by. It is rare for the self to set off and learn the art of living as an ongoing process from moment to moment, from the highest level of all — the universal. The automatic and methodical approach of the mind is what counts. Experience is the backup, its basis for acquired security, its standby ladder of tried and tested methods from which is selected the best means to proceed.

Rarely is the mind spontaneous in its response nor its interest not chained and limited to the narrow confines of the self's standing. The focus is, as much as possible, on the things that please, give pleasure or profit. Because of personal considerations the self ignores the difficult when it can unless this cannot be avoided. It has its ingrained likes and dislikes, a knack for avoiding people or situations that do not fit in with its standards. Nor is it concerned with what motivates it to behave as it does. This is not a matter of deep interest to the self so it rarely delves below the surface.

In response to the outer we follow the simple or complex directives that arise from within. There is pause for reflection only when we land into difficulties. Then the main consideration is to extricate ourselves as best we can, not to understand why the disturbances arise or what part, if any is our own contribution. Self will back pedal for preference but if it cannot avoid the issues that confront it, it will face what it must till painful times are over. Then, all being well, it will settle back into the more comfortable aspects of living, into the patterns carefully built over years of living. This, then is the main consideration of the mind — to move through life with the minimum of hindrances to the progressive flow of its own expression. Satisfying its desires, demands, likes and inclinations is the way it wants to go. And avoiding that which doesn't please it.

Briefly, that's what living is to the self. It settles into its social surrounds, accepts what it finds there, complains about the aspects that do not meet with its approval or that appear unjust, and insists on change that it agrees with. Above all, self revolves around itself and its complex desires and demands. The immediate is what concerns the self — its daily needs and appetites. Provided there is no opposition of consequence, it carries on, moving through the experiences that unfold around it. Self gives little thought to its movement and behaviour. It accepts its human face, its motion through life and the channels it travels down as it moves towards the things that attract it. The appreciation and understanding of the personality, of life and the surrounding society comes via the mind. Whatever the level of this comprehension, it is reflected in everything the self does, in the nature of what it thinks, in the conclusions it forms and the decisions made.

We grow accustomed to our own expression and accept it. If this seems odd to others who may be somewhat different in their characteristic outpouring, we continue as we are. Like a tree that is bent and shaped by the prevailing winds of the region in which it grows, so too does the self develop in the direction that expresses the inner inclinations and social input to behave and act as it does. There are powerful social trends abroad. Selective influences seep into the mind from birth. Many are intentionally inculcated along the way, firstly by parents who establish a base of rapport and a supportive background, then by the authorities who control the various aspects of the social machine.

Much of what the mind absorbs is indirect, just because it is there and there is exposure to it. The mind has a retentive capacity without really trying. Language, habits, customs, clothes, standings in the community that relate to sex are absorbed without deliberate intent. Although this content is by no means fixed and is inclined to vary and change, there are basic considerations that remain buried deep within. They become the cornerstone of our convictions about our personal lives, our country, our expectations and much we do and demand in our lives.

As a lifetime lengthens, a great deal of ground is covered in what is experienced and undertaken. Movements in many directions expand the accumulated contents and strengthen and sharpen the sense of identity and personal existence. Experience and achievement become the yardstick for measuring successful living. Add a growing accumulation of possessions and a position of status in the community and the self lifts in its standing. The family unit is one of the basic considerations and holds firm against assaults to weaken its importance. Those who grow up in and supported by family togetherness and love know its value to children and adults. The potential to enrich living is boundless and the challenges posed by intimate relationships is one of the most conducive for self learning if this is the intention.

~3~

WE ACKNOWLEDGE THE importance of much of the learning we do in life when this relates to the skills necessary to move and work in the social unit. But is self-understanding so important? In what way would we profit physically, in mental wellbeing or financially? It is easy to project illusions about self-understanding. It obviously relates to what we do, think and feel, to everything going on within and around us. The conscious is included and so too is what is termed the unconscious, that side of our nature difficult to approach. Self-understanding covers everything we are and do, the functions of the senses, the arisal of perceptions, the way we relate to others. It is an in-depth business with the basic intention of uncovering the relationship with the universal nature. Why this is so only becomes clear when this is realised. Then its value is obvious to those who break through to this spiritual dimension of existence.

The early attempts to understand revolve around the relevant information in books written by those who are spiritually awake. The reasoning capacity too is harnessed. It wouldn't allow itself to be left out anyway. But true understanding dawns when the mind rises above words and the meaning allotted to words, goes beyond ideas, even beyond the reasoning processes and touches that which is beyond. Otherwise it remains anchored on the outer fringes of what we appear to be. Stay here and the beyond doesn't reveal its nature. Self-understanding penetrates to the foundations of the activity that arises within and impresses the seeker with the need to put aside every aspect of the self. We do not move in this kind of learning until the universal enfolds us. That is the catalyst that releases a learning content that has been deep inside, ignored by the busy self as it goes on its merry way down the highway of time.

It may seem that introspection is mainly involved with self-considerations. But it rapidly expands to include the social strands that are part of the individual makeup. It moves on to cover the human expression on this planet and its place in the universal movement. The investigation that began with the emphasis on self-existence reaches out to embrace the nature of the universal existence. When mind breaks out of the chains that limit it to an individual and isolated standpoint in time it moves on to the highest standing of all — a universal one that transcends the space and time concepts that were formerly dominant.

Will it bring us back to our universal nature rather than how we are now — anchored in appearance, identified with body, name and relationships? Or will we continue to drive onwards, still puzzled, still seeking elusive final answers to the what, why and wherefore of the universal expression, ourselves included? This sought for grail of significance that seems always out of reach of the questing mind. Yet it's taken to be somewhere at the end of a long, long trail of future human endeavour.

And what of the negative side of human behaviour? The destructive side, the selfishness, the isolation, the loneliness and the emptiness, the disarrangements. Will all this vanish somewhere along the line, banished by experiment and investigation, by knowledge, by reason or by swallowing a tablet or two? Or will behaviour grow even more intractable, more complex, devious and difficult to deal with until a point is reached where we have had enough of what comes out and we long for a change? What are we after in life? Is it to continue in a human form as long as we can, to stay alive, confined in the social influences we grew up in, explore a little of our surrounds, then go on to death with the mystery posed by life left largely unsolved?

What of the creative power we hear about? When do we set to and realise this in intimate moments of discovery, so we are not left swinging in mid-air on the trapeze of belief, neither confirming the reality of its existence nor relinquishing this belief support we cling to? In my most reflective moods, the panorama of life touches me deeply. I sit, pen in hand, putting my thoughts down on paper. The words seem so inadequate in comparison to the vastness, the animation, the irrepressible movement of energy we are so much a part of. There is a deep yearning for clearer perceptions, for what is called truth, for a deeper understanding of the human expression. We wonder about God, about the purpose of life, destiny, free will, even where the human race is going — to better or worse now nuclear weapons have been invented. Will we learn the ways of peace and togetherness, create harmony in our relationships or continue to destroy our kind, the Earth and the life forms on it as we have done so often?

We have gone to the philosophers of old, the inspired prophets of the past, to the scientists, to those in the present who we take to be spiritually enlightened. We take in the words, the reasons, the explanations. No matter how inspired the expressions, the written and spoken words do not fully satisfy. There is a longing for more than mere words. We do what we can to improve our understanding but all we seem to do is travel within the confines of the self. Together with the outer that complements it, this is what we take for reality, the only one we know.

We acknowledge we were birthed in time and we know one day we will depart. Was it just a fortuitous arrangement by nature that brought us out of the obscurity of not knowing into the full light of an amazing human adventure? Such a simplistic answer is difficult to accept. When we look at all the stages the body goes through, from the tiny beginning in the womb, to birth, to the growth and development that follows, something deep inside rejects this supposition. Yet if a divine agency is involved in some way, reason demands conclusive proof so all doubts and concern for our kind are swept away in the certainty of discovery.

Living on this planet has its highlights but in many ways it has been a tragic story of suffering, starvation and violence. Must this side of human behaviour go on endlessly? There are recorded promises that it will change if we will repent of our sins (so difficult this) and return to the Great Creative Power that created all. There is also the promise that Christ will return and transform the world into goodness and light. In the meantime it is better not to dwell too much on the shocking treatment that goes on between humans. For if we did we would be constantly unhappy. Fortunate indeed are those who live in the quieter areas of the world, far from the violence and destruction going on elsewhere.

Why is it that in spite of good intentions, so much of the dark side to human behaviour surfaces? Why can't we do better and come together as a people, simply and directly expressing peace and harmony in human relationships? We are falling down badly somewhere along the line in our journey through life. Is it impossible for humans to reflect other than violence and disruption in their search for self-security? What more can people do that they haven't already tried? In international affairs, it's back to reliance on military might when all else fails. One to one relationships are often troubling. Happiness and harmony seems to be an elusive dream.

Whatever mind initiates from a self-based standpoint without spiritual input has failed to produce anything of lasting value. Every movement, freshly motivated at first, driven with enthusiastic energy, gradually bogs down in the mire of self-contradiction and conflict. Then it's back in the doldrums of intractable problems with more discussions and suggestions. Then the process takes off again. Human nature is earnest about its intentions and endeavours to improve social relationships. But it cannot seem to shift out of its habitual patterns, its self-centred standing, the constant approach that revolves around its own particular view and way of doing things. The self is too powerful to be put aside.

Any surface intention to be different is soon overridden by deep-rooted inner convictions that are the self's means of protection. With mankind shattered into separate factions, each inward-looking and stubbornly adhering to the established attitudes, a unified approach has little hope of emerging. Without spiritual understanding to dampen the forceful movement of the self, the more stubborn aspects of the self will prevail in any confrontation. Deep change is necessary in the level of understanding. The self needs to be reined in. Discipline imposed by the self from the surface is at best a stop gap. When the inner has different intentions it will inevitably break through. Anyone who has suddenly lost control could vouch for this.

That is why integrated action is needed. All aspects of the human expression functioning in unison. Separation put aside. Spiritual integration allowed its run without interference from a self that is bent on maintaining its isolated standing. This is the best kind of action — complete, unfettered action, not limited by the mind revolving around the dominance of the self and its connections.

Spiritual integration transforms the old approach, renews the self and restores the lustre that living in the old, in timeful isolation, has dulled. Living self-wrapped in time, humans grow old and worn by the constant efforts to preserve the self. They lose the sparkle of life that is reflected in the wonder and eager dance of a child. Early innocence pales before the onslaught of a multitude of experiences that hammers influences deep into an unprotected inner extent. Without spiritual input to dissolve the build-up, the inner burden grows. Sluggish then is the response of the self to the challenges that arise. The inner sensitivity is hampered by the burden, by the overlay of demanding desires and intentions. Self has broken away from its base in the spiritual strangeness, bruises and batters itself in the search for self-protection that is always threatened by change and the demands of others who are equally inclined to do likewise.

Self can wander forever in this way, or wake up and return to its spiritual homeland. In this, love is waiting. There is a host of blessings waiting — enrichment beyond its imagination. The end of limitation, of illusion and separation beckons. The end of everything disruptive and the beginning of wisdom in living. The expansive is in the air, everywhere, in the inner and the outer. Mankind can dance to the tune of the isolated self or dance with the universal music in a timeless blend of harmony. The universal heart is calling. It is time to listen. The inner is ripe with promise, ready to give birth to a new age for mankind. It has need of mankind to go forward and create the next evolutionary stage in human development. The stage is set, the directive ready. All it needs is for mankind to yield the self and go back home to claim its spiritual bonanza.

~ 4 ~

THE HUMAN STORY, in search of the spiritual strangeness, is the story of the human expression in movement, of the attempt to be free of the shackles imposed by timeful experience and social influences. Great is the torment suffered by those who reach out for perfect freedom, for the unconditioned state of Being. Here, the mind cannot go and retain any vestige of distinctive individuality or human outlook. There is so much emotional and mental upheaval as the inner begins to throw off the yoke of time and revert back to its connection with the pristine strangeness.

The storms that rage within, the strange disturbing moods that arise are difficult to define. Reasonable explanations do not ease the mind's apprehension as it senses that unplanned changes are imminent, that something out of its conscious control is taking place deep inside. From the surface it seems a silent battle is taking place between the old and the new, between the continuation of the self in the accustomed manner and the new input from the spiritual tide of life. The outcome will decide the direction the human expression travels, what values to base its movement on. The old is a composite of social influences garnered from the past, modified in the present and individual intentions projected to serve the self's deep-rooted inclinations to preserve and extend its interests.

The new direction unfolds from a reconnection with the spiritual. Its inception is beyond the vale of time and experience. Outside the conscious control of social and individual authority, it bears the stamp of divinity — its emblem of authority as it moves, through love and understanding, to take command of the human expression. Strange indeed the impact of the timeless connection. Unheralded, without fanfare, silently it happens. Swifter than a lightning flash, it's gone before "that" which receives realises what has taken place. The aftermath may be delightful, ecstatic, subdued, enlightening, even devastating if the insights released expose the inner motivations and self-centred drives of the self. The covering veneers of prejudice are shattered, illusions exposed. Eventually, as discovery deepens the depth of understanding, the mind's persistence to continue along a separate pathway of self-expansion is exhausted. The illusion creating machinery in the mind is burnt out and unable to resurrect its former capacity to cover the self's vision with defective sight. False perceptions no longer parade as the true.

The intention is to awaken the human expression to its spiritual potential; to rejuvenate the human spirit with a fresh understanding; to guide it into greener pastures of living; to expand the vision until it includes all of creation into one unified fold. We've hobbled along, crippled in outlook, suffering delusions of grandeur because of technological advances in so many directions. Inwardly, spiritually, we've hardly moved. We still find it very difficult to live in harmony with each other and to share what we produce. Fabulous wealth for some, want and hardship for many. Communication between people remains mostly on the verbal level. Rarely do words bring people together, or inspire a fundamental change in human relationships. There is access to volumes of printed matter, to the accumulated wisdom from the past and the knowledge gained along the way. All this we draw from to improve the quality of life.

So many specialists deal with our difficulties and problems. The products from an expanding technology appear thick and fast in the social marketplace. Living, for those who can afford it, has become a progression of bright, shiny, complex gadgets. They surround us on all sides and they are the measure of human progress. See how far we have developed from our caveman days, when hunting for food was by club or spear and reading and writing were not yet given birth.

Now, we live in caves of a different kind. Still isolated, still wary of others not in the same national fold, with different lifestyles, political ideologies or religious ways. Unease and concern continues. International attempts fail to bring about peace everywhere or economic conditions that apply equally to all and leave no one on the outside of the prosperity window, looking in, wanting a share of material abundance. There is apprehension about divisions that surface, the way of economic development, the natural environment, changes and policies that leaders want to implement, the education system and its intentions. The media too comes in for a share of criticism and above all there remains the perennial question, "Where are we going?"

In the social sphere, a distinctive and secure standing draws strongly. Many will work like beavers, re-educating themselves if need be to bring this about. The benefits modern social arrangements bring are obvious. So too are the side effects. We enjoy the benefits and energetically apply ourselves in the chosen directions to supply what we need and desire. What we have, we do not want to lose. In fact, we prefer to add to this via a productive outpouring to improve the quality of life. We rely on political arrangements to take care of our interests and as a protection from undue disturbances that threaten to undermine the stability of our lifestyles.

Is the main intention to continue along the directions decided by social directives, dealing with the problems that arise and maintaining the social unit as an ongoing concern until an efficient production machine has been created that caters for every foreseeable contingency? Will people remain isolated behind national walls, separated by unbridgeable chasms from those who are likewise enclosed within different and apparently alien mental fortresses, lifestyles and customs? Where will the impetus come from to change centuries-old, deep-rooted attitudes and revered institutions that keep people anchored in separation? The past is a reflection of the way humans have travelled. It served a useful purpose then. Now, much of it is an impediment that prevents mankind functioning in a unified manner, deeply established in its spiritual nature.

Are people ready to put aside the restricted social flow they are accustomed to and enlarge its basis to include all mankind under one unified banner? And, in reaching out for the spiritual togetherness that moves people in harmony, what arrangements would they opt for and support without resistance or reservations as to their value? A common political and religious basis does not appear likely. These have become more fragmented with the passage of time. The advent of new social ideas has won widespread support for a time, particularly from the downtrodden and oppressed if these offer an improvement in their condition.

Whatever is offered to a hungry, needy or dissatisfied people, not yet has a single arrangement won complete acceptance from the inhabitants of this planet. Mankind continues, as divided as ever and stubbornly opposed to anything that may seemingly threaten the familiar social arrangements. Change is constantly with us, yet there is often uncertainty when this affects the self. Too much disturbance is not wanted. Anything that asks for more than people are prepared to give lacks the necessary support to be effective. We prefer to coast along the highway of life, enjoying ourselves according to individual inclinations. We gravitate towards the things, the pursuits that offer the kind of returns we seek from day to day living. And if trouble did not rear its disturbing head in some way — economic and relationship breakdowns, eruptions of violence — then we would quite happily go on as we are until death do us part from this life we know so well.

It is perhaps the variety and extent of the difficulties that surface, the conflicts, the erratic behaviour, the breakdowns, the intractable problems that arise that bring us down to earth with a jolt. This may lead to a serious reflection on the individual role, the organisations we rely on, even where we are headed if we continue along the same pathways that have so often led to temporary and unproductive dead ends or even worse. We may begin to wonder, not only what is wrong with our leaders but also with ourselves — whether as individuals, with very little power, we can do something, anything to improve the situation in our part of the world. Not the something that is stop gap aid, which may lead to an amelioration of existing conditions, but gets down to the grass roots. That is, the removal of one troublesome centre around the place (the self) and replace this with an awakened expression that contributes harmony, rather than otherwise, to the social climate.

Having decided that a transformation is necessary for our wellbeing, even for our continued existence on this planet, and declared the intention to commit oneself, what steps can be taken which could guarantee a successful conclusion to this worthy endeavour? On every side, those who want support for their particular ventures and organisations offer promises of great rewards or worthwhile returns if we follow the guidelines they lay down for us — the proverbial red carpet to inner riches. In return, we give our allegiance to a person, to the authority of a system, a collection of ideas or a particular arrangement of doing things. Some of these people flash out of obscurity, blaze brightly for a time, then they and what they stand for collapses just as quickly, leaving disillusionment, confusion and bewilderment in the wake of their passing.

Meanwhile, the many demands of life continue and people move their steady way down the crowded highway of life. What goes on inside, what they experience and think about it all, they alone are in a position to observe, to learn and do something about, should they be inclined. People need to be strongly motivated to move in a new direction. The driving force may be discontent, the desire to reach out for the spiritual stars when they hear about this. Constant suffering may be a spur, emotional and mental upheavals, or maybe they move because they feel that something of importance is still missing in spite of all that today's social arrangements have to offer.

Once the decision is made that the spiritual is the way to go, the need for guidelines to move along may cause some degree of difficulty. Mind cannot envisage movement towards a goal without self-involvement applied along particular lines or as a composite of a program of action with the self as the central figure. This may involve disciplines, meditation, change of routines and lifestyles and reading the books on spirituality that appeal. Those who acknowledge the need for a deep change no longer expect this to come from the political spectrum, from national and organisational leaders. Nor is it expected that the mind, using a base of experience, intention and knowledge can do this on its own. If this were so, we would surely be rapidly improving the human climate on the planet, with the indicator on the barometer moving steadily over to fair and heading in the fine direction.

This is not the case and although there are places not overloaded with serious troubles, for many insecurity, oppression, violence, starvation and a lack of the necessities of life prevail. Even though we energetically pursue the preservation and expansion of the self's social position, may have accumulated much in the way of material possessions and live a very busy and satisfying life, is life a fun-filled journey, free of inner deterioration? Are we overflowing with the spiritual, open to its passage, allowing it through without self-interference? Are we jaded, overloaded with concerns, with too much to do? Are we harried from within and without? Is there an inner restlessness, the constant drive for more and more in every direction?

These are the indicators that the spiritual is neglected, that the self has taken over with its manipulative ways, breeding concerns, fears, ambitions — so much mischief it gets up to. With the self abroad, it fills the centre stage of life and the wonder and mystery of the spiritual strangeness is neglected. Without this discovery, there is no chance for transformation, for an end to the dominance of the self and the emergence of a spiritual renaissance. We drift along like dreamers, lost in our dreams. They turn at times into nightmares. We need to step out of the limited self into the expansive, the unlimited — to let go of everything that holds us back to self and timeful experience.

The difficulty is that self is caught up with everything that flows before the conscious vision. This is its view of reality. Ask it to let go of all that appears to be and it is lost. How can it let go of itself? This fills the conscious viewpoint to overflowing. The mind's business is in time, to deal with the movement of time, not with the timeless. This is beyond it. The interaction of separate selves does not exist in the timeless.

Above all, it wants to hold on to itself, to some kind of identifiable experience as an observer. In this its existence is assured. Mind wants to trap the timeless in its own fold, make of it some kind of experience it can apprehend. It uses a typically surface approach in its attempts to discover that which is unknown. It goes to the routines and suggestions offered by the enlightened ones. It will do anything as long as results are assured. The enlightened ones well understand the nature of the mind and its capabilities. They understand the role of effort, what it can and can't do. Give the mind a role to play, set it on its way and it will move heaven and earth to succeed.

If the mind could break free of the restrictions that enclose it by effort, its movement towards the universal nature would be easy. But the restrictions that blind the mind and prevent true perception go too deep for effort to eradicate. Effort applied by a limited mind yields limited results. Effort to understand is a creation of a limited mind, not of a self established in the universal strangeness. What it does is focus the mind along a narrow channel of endeavour. Conceived by the limited, nurtured along the way by the limited, in the end it dawns on the mind that it is going nowhere special. That's if it is perceptive enough not to be deceived for a lifetime.

Yet effort serves this useful purpose. Applied till it wearies the mind of its concentrated attempts to go beyond, mind lets go. Not only on the surface, right throughout its nature. Projection from the self ceases. Completely. Spontaneously. It is unbelievably simple when it happens. Contrived effort doesn't come into it. Seeking stops. These words describe a happening that cannot be thought of. It is total — stillness beyond description. Awareness of self shifts back to universal awareness without a centre to observe, to know, to experience. For a moment mind is lost and knows not where it is or what it is. Then it's back in time but it's picked up something along the way. An instant awareness of what eventuated. This it transmits into thought.

Words however have variable meanings. The understanding that listens will do with them what it will. When this is based on discovery, all is well. Meaning will not be transposed. While the mind without self-discovery is abroad giving reign to a complex intellect to express meaning, obscurity rather than clarity prevails. Light is absent. The feeble light of the mind takes over, the surface view is taken to be the all.

Mind loves to wander in complex translations, not dwell simply in the reality of "What Is". Realisation stills the chattering tongue, brings light into a life where formerly degrees of darkness ruled. Without the understanding, the insights that follow discovery, the human expression is but a shadow inwardly of what it should be. The passage of the human ship over the seas of time is a troubled one.

With no clear directive at the helm the ship is unsure of its direction, unable to call at the ports of peace, harmony and togetherness. The motive power is disarranged, disconnected from the universal source. There are many captains at the wheel, each going in different directions, so the human fleet is in disarray, the sails not filled with the spiritual winds that stir from beyond the vale of time.

The ports of call are discord, economic troubles, violence, unseemly behaviour, war, starvation and want — a medley of seemingly insurmountable difficulties and intractable problems. All this created by humans who have lost touch with the spiritual strangeness, who have tried to go it alone using the usual resources of logical reason. Were humans in harmony with the spiritual, their steps would be sure. They would proceed on the solid foundations of an awakened understanding. This would carry them through the vicissitudes of life with serenity and calm purpose. None of the surface differences extant today would be permitted to mar the integrated approach that living in the spiritual inevitably brings.

The intellect, with its commander in chief logical reason, now the dominant ruler on the human throne and sole arbiter of the direction in which humans travel and the social arrangements they live by, will yield this authority to a power and wisdom greater than its own. It will not yield in a hurry, may even be reluctant, but inevitably the full force of an awakened spiritual understanding will dissolve its former standing as the number one in human affairs. It yields because it must, because there are no other options available to it that seem better. Such is the nature of the wisdom displayed and the quality of the love bestowed.

Many are the accolades heaped on the intellect by impressed populations. Many the adornments of achievements and construction garnered along the way. People revere its authoritative utterances. With the spiritual acknowledged as all important, all that's left for it is to serve, to be a go-between, a reflective prism that conveys a light from beyond. Not that the intellect will mind for it gains the benefits of spiritual blessings beyond description. They are considerable and affect every strata of the human expression. Above all, there is the inner awakening that dawns like the rising of the sun and gradually ascends to its noonday zenith. This is maintained unhindered by any interference from the lesser self whose breakaway movement and isolationist endeavours obscured the spiritual and denied it egress into its surface movement.

With the dawning and development of this awakening, humans begin to live to the maximum extent of their endowed capacity. An endowment gifted by the supreme One — a sharing of its bountiful and mysterious nature with its human children. We belong to the Sunshine of Being. Its nature is our very own. The transplant we identify with, the body, emotions and thinking side are the surface reflection, the means for the inner sensitivity to operate from a central position in a space/time related environment.

Those who decide to dedicate their lives to spiritual discovery proceed to set up guidelines. These are devised from books, from contact with spiritual centres. They revolve around emotional and mental disciplines, meditation and reflective analysis on the nature of experience and behaviour. Whether all this is an effective aid or otherwise is of little consideration in the beginning. Self-involvement is the main concern — generating movement that is an encouragement and a reassurance that self is on its way to heaven.

The new arrangements are superimposed on those that previously existed. The adopted transplants are carefully cultivated by the mind and self willingly settles into the projected patterns. Initially, satisfaction rules the human roost. There is the conviction that the self is on the way to the spiritual strangeness, to the nature that will yield the understanding and insights that clarify the mystery of life and the universe and take the self deep into the mind and how it operates from its base as the central "I". This understanding is expected to yield complete truth, not a partial or limited one. Something that survives the test of time and experience and is not negated by changes that follow.

Union with the strangeness is to be the basis for the mind's approach and although it will still base much of this on experience and social influences, nothing will be permitted to disrupt the directives that flow from spiritual union. This is paramount. Such are some of the expectations built up from information gathered from those who have travelled the timeless way to the heart's desire. They vary with the considerations of those involved in the search.

Spiritual enlightenment is a difficult undertaking. Barriers projected by the mind arise at every turn. The unfolding is one of facing the barriers, the mental blockages projected by the self from its isolated and separatist standing. They are never ending, these projections. Always there is another facet to the mind's capacity to rearrange its base and continue along the way, down the highway of time as an entity of purpose intent on further discovery and self-achievement. The insights that flow in when spiritual integration is effected serve to check the self's expansion for a time. But the mind has the capacity to rise anew, to re-establish its forward movement towards whatever attracts it and before long it is swinging down the pathway of establishing the self wherever it will. Until such time as insight strikes again with its incisive clarity and its devious, self-centred ways are again exposed.

A spiritual unfolding is largely a private matter. No matter how much self may meet and mix with others, no one else can journey through that inner domain that is the private precinct of the self. Nor can others understand what is unfolding unless they too have travelled inwards towards the Silent Heart. Even then, the background they travel through, even if similar in some respects, will vary because of the differences in standing and experiences between one background and another.

Of the similarities — everyone strives for security and enjoyment each in one's own way. The drive by the mind to accumulate operates by and large in everyone. Likewise, avoiding disturbance and pain is common to all and the deep urge to continue self-existence is deeply rooted indeed. The reactions of the mind to experience often have similarities. When the self leaves the accustomed field of social travel to delve into its inner workings, here too, there is much that is the same in the way humans react once discovery has made its impact and the mind does what it will with what it learns from the new happenings.

There is never any pressure brought by the inner to prevent any course of action the mind is bent on. Pre-discovery, mind acts from experience, through reason, desire, choice or need. Fear is often a deterrent that spurs the self to avoid the things it would rather not face. With the coming of the spiritual, the basic determinant in the self's movement through life undergoes subtle changes. Immediately afterwards, a fresh flowing impetus, charged with energy, clear in perception and understanding makes its presence felt. It surges to express its nature, carrying the individual expression along with the enthusiastic tide of its movement. The song and dance that breaks out is irresistible and spontaneous.

The cluttered approach of the mind is brushed aside. Limitation is shattered by a universal tide. Something immeasurably vast has swept aside the isolated mainstream of the self, dissolved the barriers that kept it at bay and denied it an outlet. Self sings to new vibrations. The heart bursts into new life. Exquisite feelings arise and the joy is boundless. What a shame it doesn't last. Mind is too persistent in its movement. The roots of the self go deep. It does not yield with one impact, nor with several, nor with many. Stubborn indeed is its desire to persist in a self-made mould. I am me. I must be as an individual of distinction. What a driving force for continuity.

The Eternal has none of this clutter in its nature. Distinction is for dreaming. It's delightful when pain is not. But it's the dreamtime of living. Mind loves the dream. Here it can be someone, do something, climb the dizzy heights of self-achievement. The Eternal means self-extinction, as a someone special, as a face, form, figure — all the fun of time's fair. When the dream is over, what then? Life may seem long but it is brief. And death draws down the curtain on this side of time's Great Divide.

Why then shrink from the Eternal? Why not set out to discover this now and learn the true meaning of death? It is the end of the self as an individual but it is not the extinction of *What Is*. That remains untouched. The *What Is* is the source of what appears, of the dream we share. The dream covers *What Is*. The watcher is fascinated by the movement, identified with the appearance. It loses touch with its own immortal nature. Until someone knocks on the door of the mind and reminds it of its spiritual heritage. The perceptive ones respond. They pack their bags and go, just as they are. Nor will they rest, nor find peace until they are selflessly ensconced deep in the heart of the Timeless Strangeness.

They are the blessed, for they lodge in that which is never ending. Here they sleep the universal sleep, untouched by time and decay. They live beyond the dream, yet as the universal, they are the dream and everything in it. There is only the One. Always it has been so. It is now. Always it will be. There is no other truth of such consequence.

About the author

JOSEPH RAFFA WAS born in 1927 in Fremantle, Western Australia. He enjoyed an idyllic childhood roaming the bush and the seashore. In his teens Joseph became a dedicated atheist, looking to science for answers to the riddles of life and the universe. Then, in his early twenties, he experienced a moment of discovery that transformed his life. As Joseph's life opened out spiritually following this awakening, he was inspired to put pen to paper to encourage others to embark on their own journey of discovery.

Joseph died of cancer in 2010, leaving behind a legacy of inspirational writing which is now being made available to a wider audience. Visit www.towardsthesilentheart.com for more information about Joseph and his books.

Look for other books
by Joseph Raffa

Beside Still Waters
ISBN 9780987227676

This beautiful collection of essays touches on the universal search for meaning and inspires readers to reach out for the still waters of the spirit.

The human heart longs for peace and harmony. It seeks a restful haven from the relentless busyness of everyday life, drawing us to spend tranquil moments in natural surrounds that offer a brief respite from the hustle and bustle. There is a state of inner stillness, when the endless chatter of the mind has ceased, that a deeper understanding arises. These are the 'still waters' that bring new life to mankind, that lay claim to the heart and redirect the mind. These are the waters of peace, love and true togetherness that lift us up to divine heights of being and living.

The Silent Guardian
ISBN 9780987227669

A timely reminder of our spiritual journey and true purpose on Earth.

Joseph shares an inspirational message for those who care to listen.

'Explore the planets, the outer reaches of space, the depths of the seas. Burrow into the earth, climb every mountain. When you have seen it all, you will still be left with the mystery of yourself. Turn and face this. Explore this. When you've travelled the extent and depth of the human expression, much of what you learn will be beyond the mind's capacity to convey through verbalisation. When heart speaks to heart, what more is there to say?' *-The Silent Guardian*

Beyond the Cross
The Christ Collection
ISBN 9780987227652

A moving collection of inspired pieces about Jesus.

Joseph Raffa was a dedicated atheist when he set out in search of answers to the riddles of life and the universe. Then, in a blissful moment of discovery, the God the Bible speaks of, the Allah of Mohammed and the longed for Nirvana of the Buddhists came into his life.

As his life opened out spiritually, Joseph began to have a deeper appreciation of Jesus, His life and His role in the spiritual awakening of Mankind. Visions and insights arose unbidden, in such a manner that their authenticity could not be questioned. The young man who was an atheist for a time, who cared not to read the Bible or take much notice of Christ and His life, found himself anchored in God and also writing pieces extolling the virtues, the wisdom and the love expressed by that super spiritual being of long ago.

www.ingramcontent.com/pod-product-compliance
Lightning Source LLC
Chambersburg PA
CBHW060707030426
42337CB00017B/2789